Bugs

Weta

by Trudy Becker

FOCUS READERS
PIONEER

www.focusreaders.com

Focus Readers is distributed by North Star Editions:
sales@northstareditions.com | 888-417-0195

Produced for Focus Readers by Red Line Editorial.

Photographs ©: Shutterstock Images, cover, 1, 6, 10, 14, 18, 20; iStockphoto, 4, 8, 17; Chris Winks/Wikimedia, 12

Library of Congress Cataloging-in-Publication Data
Names: Becker, Trudy, author.
Title: Weta / by Trudy Becker.
Description: Lake Elmo, MN : Focus Readers, 2023. | Series: Bugs | Includes index. | Audience: Grades 2-3
Identifiers: LCCN 2022035861 (print) | LCCN 2022035862 (ebook) | ISBN 9781637394540 (hardcover) | ISBN 9781637394915 (paperback) | ISBN 9781637395646 (pdf) | ISBN 9781637395288 (ebook)
Subjects: LCSH: Wetas--Juvenile literature.
Classification: LCC QL506 .B43 2023 (print) | LCC QL506 (ebook) | DDC 595.7/26--dc23/eng/20220818
LC record available at https://lccn.loc.gov/2022035861
LC ebook record available at https://lccn.loc.gov/2022035862

Printed in the United States of America
Mankato, MN
012023

About the Author

Trudy Becker lives in Minneapolis, Minnesota. She likes exploring new places and loves anything involving books.

Table of Contents

Chapter 1

Out of Sight

The sun is going down. Night is coming. A weta crawls out of a hole. It was hiding all day. But now it's time to move.

Weta are insects. There are many different types of weta. They all live in New Zealand. Some live in trees. Some live in caves. And some live on the ground.

Fun Fact

Giant weta are called *wetapunga*. That means "god of ugly things."

Chapter 2

Weta Bodies

A weta has six legs. It also has three main body parts. It has a head. It has a **thorax** in the middle. And it has an **abdomen** at the back.

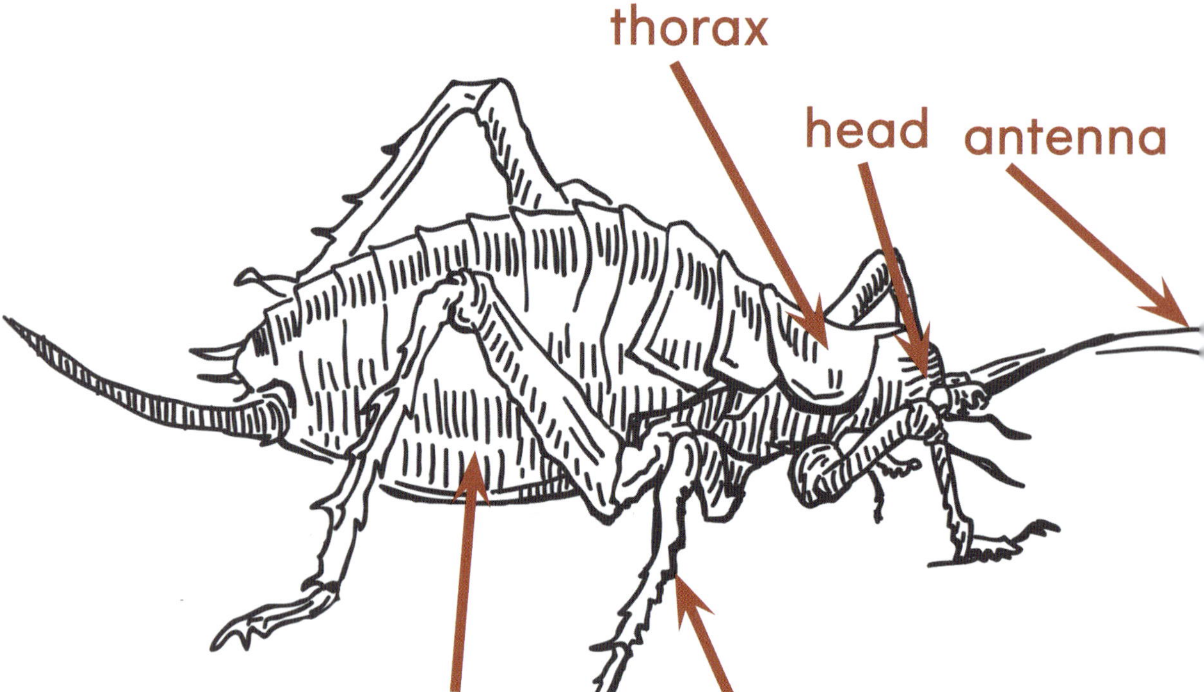
thorax
head
antenna
abdomen
leg

All weta have **antennae** to sense things. But not all weta look the same. They are different sizes. Some have long, thin antennae. Other weta have strong legs for jumping far.

Fun Fact

Weta have ears behind their knees.

Chapter 3

Weta Strengths

Some weta have **tusks**. The tusks come out of their jaws. But the tusks aren't for biting. Weta use them to fight. They push their enemies with the tusks.

If weta are in danger, they try to defend themselves. They can stretch their back legs. They show their spines. That scares or scratches **predators**.

Fun Fact

Giant weta are the biggest kind of weta. They can weigh more than mice.

Rat Danger

In the past, weta did not have many predators. But then, rats came to their **habitats**. Rats can easily smell weta. Rats hunt them. Now, some weta are **endangered**. People are trying to help. They make safe areas where weta can live.

Chapter 4

Weta Life

Weta eat lots of different foods. Many are **omnivores**. Some weta eat insects. Many weta eat leaves. Other weta can eat fruit or seeds. Giant weta eat carrots, too.

ovipositor

Female weta have parts called **ovipositors**. They use them to lay eggs. Weta put eggs deep in the soil. Later, the eggs hatch. It can take two years for an egg to grow into an adult.

Fun Fact

Many weta live in holes or tunnels.

FOCUS ON

Weta

Write your answers on a separate piece of paper.

1. Write a sentence that explains the main idea of Chapter 4.
2. Weta live in New Zealand. What insects live near your home?
3. What is the middle part of a weta's body?
   - A. wing
   - B. abdomen
   - C. thorax
4. Why is soil a safe place for weta to lay eggs?
   - A. Soil makes the eggs taste bad.
   - B. Soil hides the eggs from predators.
   - C. Predators are afraid of soil.

Answer key on page 24.

Glossary

abdomen
The back part of an insect. It contains the heart and stomach.

antennae
Long, thin body parts on an insect's head. The parts are used for sensing.

endangered
In danger of dying out.

habitats
Places where animals live.

omnivores
Animals that eat both meat and plants to survive.

ovipositors
Body parts used by female insects to lay eggs.

predators
Animals that hunt other animals for food.

thorax
The middle part of an insect. The legs are attached to this part.

tusks
Long, pointed teeth that stick out from the faces of some animals.

To Learn More

BOOKS

Levy, Janey. *Giant Wetas Shock!* New York: Gareth Stevens Publishing, 2018.

Schuh, Mari. *Cricket or Grasshopper?* Minneapolis: Bellwether Media, 2022.

NOTE TO EDUCATORS

Visit **www.focusreaders.com** to find lesson plans, activities, links, and other resources related to this title.

Index

Answer Key: 1. Answers will vary; **2.** Answers will vary; **3.** C; **4.** B